pectoral fins

Longfin makos are similar to shortfins, but they have longer pectoral fins and darker coloring around their mouths. They swim in the same tropical and **temperate** seas as shortfins. However, they are often found at greater depths.

The mako is the fastest shark in the ocean. It can reach speeds of more than 40 miles (64 kilometers) per hour. The mako has two **dorsal fins**. They help the shark keep its balance. The pectoral fins let it steer. The mako sways its powerful tail fin from side to side to move forward. It often builds up speed and leaps out of the water to heights of up to 20 feet (6 meters)!

Mako skeletons are made of **cartilage** instead of bone. This lets makos bend and turn quickly when they chase prey. The mako's body is covered with **dermal denticles**. These tough scales are made of the same material as teeth. They protect the shark from injury and help it move

# MAKO SHARK
## TRACKED

In the fall and winter, many makos **migrate** long distances across the ocean to search for food and give birth in warmer waters. Scientists have tracked makos traveling over 2,500 miles (4,025 kilometers). Many makos return to the same places every year.

Makos are found from the surface to depths of 2,430 feet (740 meters). They hunt near the surface at night and in deeper water during the day. Unlike most other fish, the mako can keep its body temperature warmer than the surrounding water. This helps power the shark's muscles and increase its strength and speed. This also lets the mako swim in cooler waters to hunt for prey.

= mako shark territory

The adult mako is an **apex predator**. Its favorite foods include tuna, swordfish, and herring. It also devours squid, sea turtles, and even other sharks. The mako uses its strong senses to hunt. It has a keen sense of smell, and its large eyes can find prey in dark waters. Sensors called **lateral lines** run the length of the shark's body. They feel the movements of nearby prey. The mako also has sensors called **ampullae of Lorenzini** on its snout. These detect the **electric fields** of animals and lead the shark to prey. A mako's teeth bend inward. This helps the shark hold on to struggling prey.

13

## TRADING TEETH

The Māori people of New Zealand traded mako teeth and wore them as jewelry.

The mako is **ovoviviparous**. Pups develop in eggs that hatch inside the mother's **uterus**. The hatched young eat unhatched eggs and smaller pups in the uterus. Mothers give birth after 15 to 18 months. Most litters have 8 to 10 pups, but some have as many as 18 or as few as 4. Larger mothers tend to have more pups.

At birth, pups are about 24 inches (61 centimeters) long and can swim alone. Males **mature** when they are about 8 years old. At this time, they are usually around 6.5 feet (2 meters) in length. Females mature when they are about 18 years old and around 9 feet (2.7 meters) long.

young mako shark

## COUNT THE YEARS

Scientists determine a mako's age by counting the growth rings in its backbone. Some scientists estimate their life span to be over 30 years.

# MAKO SHARK
## CURRENT STATUS

The mako is a prized **game fish**. Sport fishers enjoy the challenge and excitement of catching this active shark. After it is hooked on a fishing line, the mako is famous for leaping out of the water. Its strong fighting spirit can be dangerous. Makos have been known to charge boats. Some even leap into them and damage the boats or injure the fishers.

Makos have also caused serious injury to swimmers and divers. Several attacks have even resulted in death. Though people who swim or dive in mako territory must be careful, encounters are rare. Makos are usually found in the deep ocean.

The mako population is not yet in danger, but scientists worry about its future. The International Union for Conservation of Nature (IUCN) has given the mako a **vulnerable** rating. Its meat is considered one of the tastiest shark meats. It is also fished for its fins in parts of Asia. Scientists fear that people could **overfish** the shark.

The mako faces other threats. It is often caught as **bycatch** in nets and on fishing lines. Some fishers are making changes to protect the mako. They traditionally use wire to connect fishing line to hooks. Many now use **nylon**. When makos are caught as bycatch, they can bite through the nylon and escape to freedom.

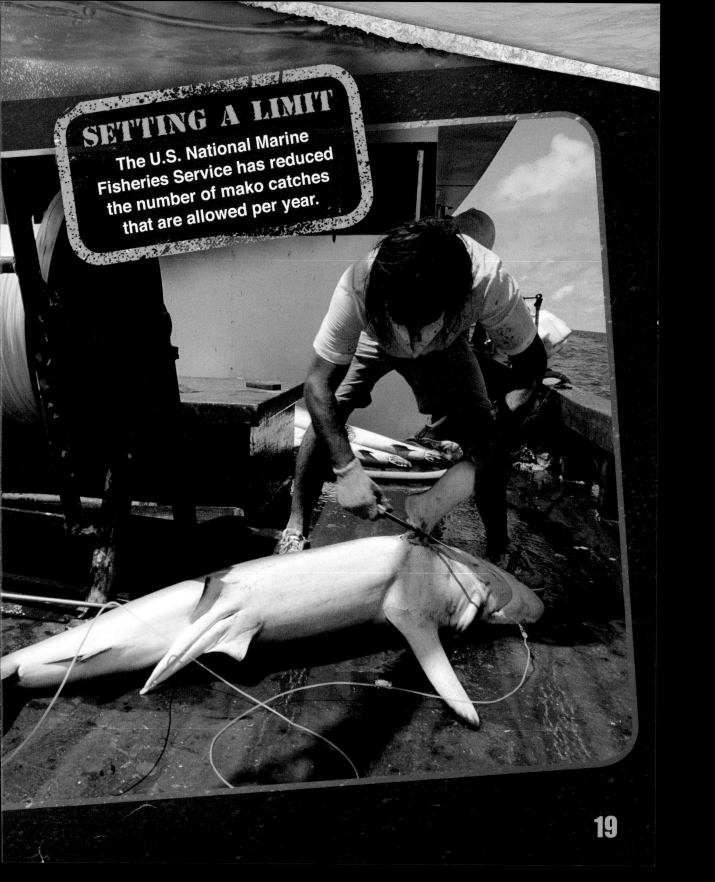

## SETTING A LIMIT

The U.S. National Marine Fisheries Service has reduced the number of mako catches that are allowed per year.

# SHARK BRIEF

**Common Name:** Mako Shark

**Also Known As:** Blue Pointer

**Claim to Fame:** Fastest and highest-leaping shark

**Hot Spots:**
California
Hawaii
East Africa
Gulf of Mexico
Red Sea
New Zealand

**Life Span:** 30 years or more

**Current Status:** Vulnerable (IUCN)

EXTINCT

EXTINCT IN THE WILD

CRITICALLY ENDANGERED

ENDANGERED

VULNERABLE

NEAR THREATENED

LEAST CONCERN

Makos have an important role in the ocean. They help keep prey populations under control. They also eat weak and sick animals. The strongest prey can escape sharks and live on to give birth. Makos also help clean the oceans by eating dead animals and garbage.

Scientists still have much to learn about the mako. This active shark does not do well in captivity. Researchers must study it in the wild. They have learned that many mako sharks give birth off the coast of southern California. This information could help protect mako mothers and pups from fishers. As more people take an interest in the mako's survival, the speedy shark is sure to thrive!

# GLOSSARY

**ampullae of Lorenzini**—a network of tiny jelly-filled sacs around a shark's snout; the jelly is sensitive to the electric fields of nearby prey.

**apex predator**—a predator that is not hunted by any other animal

**bycatch**—animals that are accidentally caught with fishing nets or lines

**cartilage**—firm, flexible connective tissue that makes up a shark's skeleton

**dermal denticles**—small, tooth-like scales that cover some types of fish

**dorsal fins**—the fins on the back of a fish

**electric fields**—waves of electricity created by movement; every living being has an electric field.

**game fish**—a fish caught for sport

**lateral lines**—a system of tubes beneath a shark's skin that helps it detect changes in water pressure

**mature**—to become able to reproduce

**migrate**—to move from one place to another, often with the seasons

**nylon**—a material made of strong, flexible fibers

**overfish**—to greatly reduce the number of fish in an area by fishing too much

**ovoviviparous**—producing young that develop in eggs inside the body; ovoviviparous animals give birth to live young.

**pectoral fins**—a pair of fins that extend from each side of a fish's body

**temperate**—neither too warm nor too cold

**uterus**—a protective chamber inside some female animals; mako sharks develop in eggs inside the mother's uterus.

**vulnerable**—at risk of becoming endangered

# TO LEARN MORE

## At the Library

Burnham, Brad. *The Mako Shark*. New York, N.Y.: PowerKids Press, 2001.

Klein, Adam G. *Mako Sharks*. Edina, Minn.: Abdo Pub., 2006.

Randolph, Joanne. *The Mako Shark: Built for Speed*. New York, N.Y.: PowerKids Press, 2007.

## On the Web

Learning more about mako sharks is as easy as 1, 2, 3.

1. Go to www.factsurfer.com.

2. Enter "mako sharks" into the search box.

3. Click the "Surf" button and you will see a list of related Web sites.

With factsurfer.com, finding more information is just a click away.

# INDEX